I Can Do All Things
Philippians 4:13
a Memory Verse Kids™ book

I AM Unlimited Publishing
Hummelstown, Pennsylvania 17036

Copyright ©2013 Krystena Lee. Memory Verse Kids is a Trademark of Krystena Lee. All rights reserved. Printed in the U.S.A. No part of this book may be used or reproduced in any manner whatsoever without written permission from the publisher except in the case of brief quotations embodied in critical articles and reviews

ISBN: 978-0-9890581-1-7

"'I can do all things through Christ who strengthens me!'—Philippians 4:13," Little Dave said as he jumped up and got dressed.

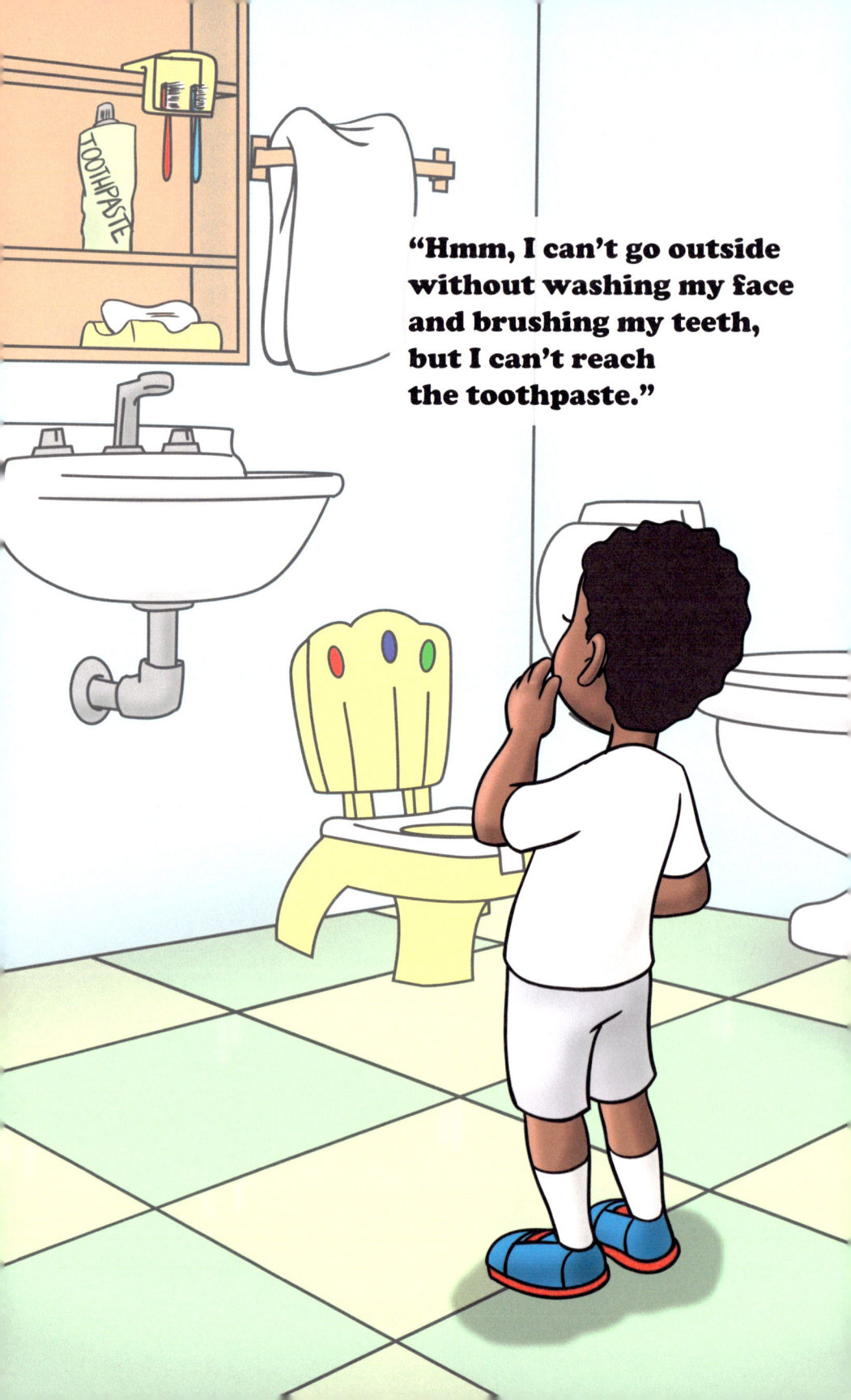

Little Dave looked down at his tummy and said, "Uh-oh, looks like you need to get ready for our big day too."

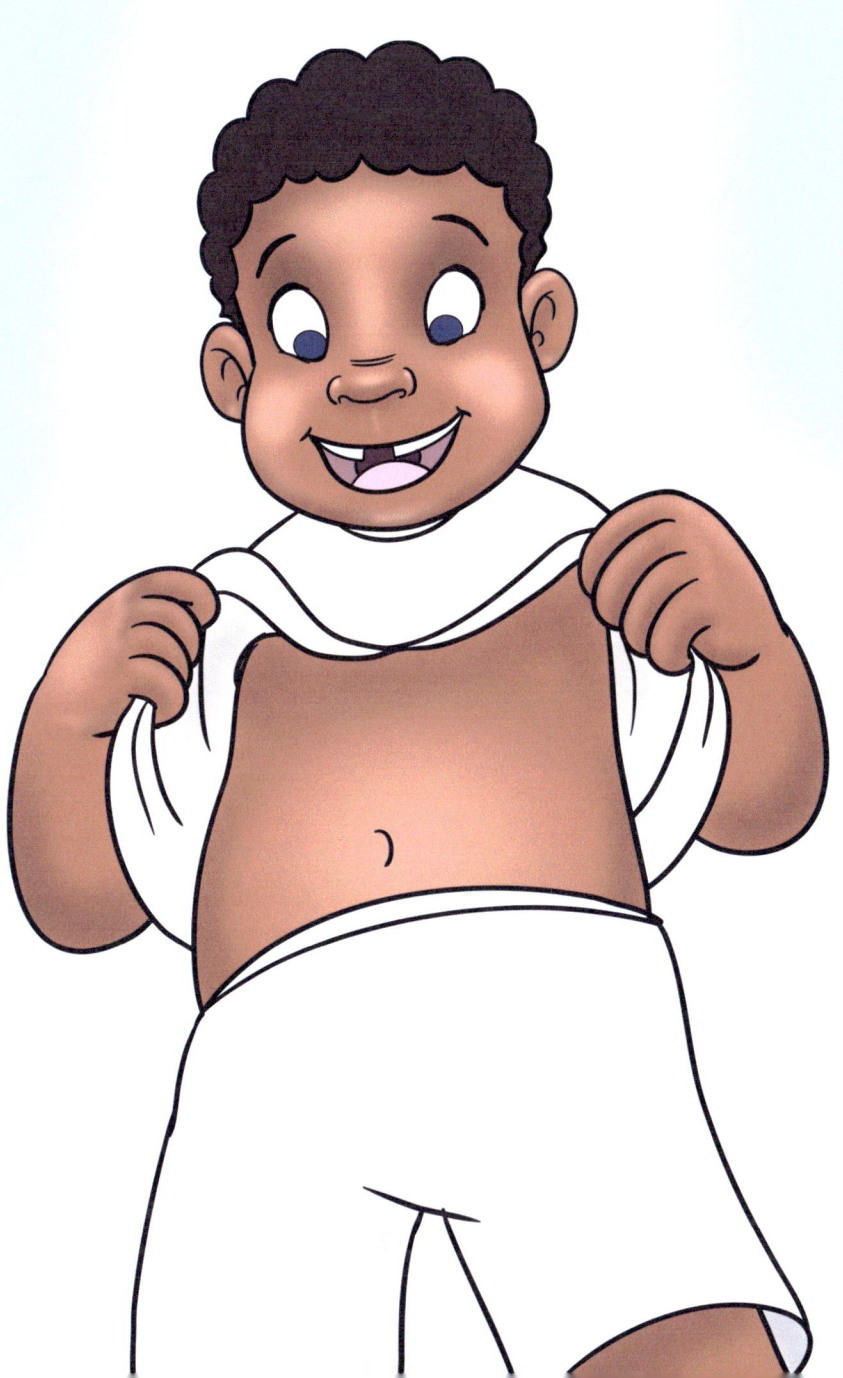

Little Dave remembered his Sunday school lesson again and repeated it out loud, "'I can do all things through Christ who strengthens me!'—Philippians 4:13." He chose some fruit from the bowl on the table and made some toast.

When he finished his breakfast, he was ready for action!

Little Dave ran into his parents' room, saying, "Today is the big day! We are going to take my training wheels off. And I am ready to ride!"

Soon Little Dave and his daddy made their way into the garage and took the training wheels off of Little Dave's bike.

But he didn't get very far.

"I don't think I can do it, Daddy," Little Dave said.

Little Dave's Daddy hugged him tight and said, "Don't give up, son. Just remember Philippians 4:13."

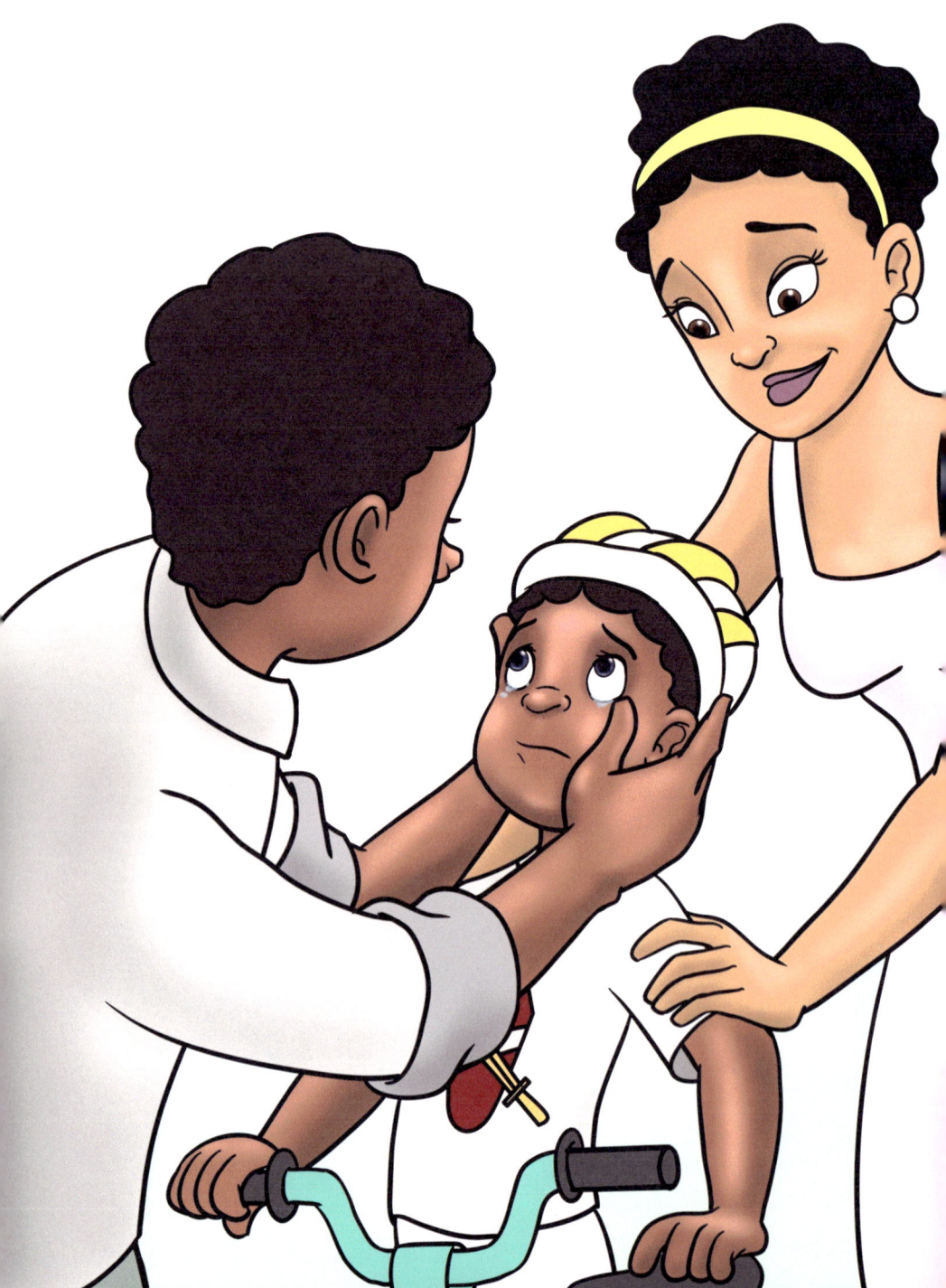

"'I can do all things through Christ who strengthens me!'" Little Dave shouted as he got back on his bike and began to pedal.

First Little Dave pedaled past the mailbox.

When he passed the giant oak tree at the corner, he turned around and rode back.

"Did you see me, Daddy? I did it! I didn't fall down. 'I can do all things through Christ who strengthens me!'—Philippians 4:13."

From then on, Little Dave knew anything was possible with Jesus, and he told everyone he knew.

"I can do all things through Christ who strengthens me." —Philippians 4:13

Made in United States
Cleveland, OH
08 May 2025